CERNE'S G
and Village Guide

Text by **Rodney Legg**
Photographs by **Colin Graham**

Dorset Publishing Company dpc
at the WINCANTON PRESS
National School, North Street, Wincanton, Somerset BA9 9AT

Second edition, revised and expanded 1990. International Standard Book Number 0 948699 17 5. Text copyright Rodney Legg © 1986-90. Photographs copyright Dorset Publishing Company and Colin Graham © 1986. First edition published as International Standard Book Number 0 902129 76 7. This edition typeset by Timmy Taylor and Reg Ward, for SOS, Shaftesbury, and Wordstream, Poole, with bromides of illustrations by Stuart Rougvie at FWB Printing, Wincanton, and layouts by Rodney Legg. "Cerne Walks" were put into a usable state in 1990 by Mr Thomas of the Rights of Way office at Dorset County Council, Dorchester, with commendable alacrity following complaints about blockages from the Open Spaces Society. Printed in Great Britain by Dotesios Limited at Kennet Way, Trowbridge, Wiltshire, and distributed by Dorset Publishing Company from Wincanton Press, National School, North Street, Wincanton, Somerset BA9 9AT, telephone 0963 32583 or 0963 34292

Also by Rodney Legg

Editor *Dorset – the county magazine* [issues 1 to 114, 1968-87]
Purbeck Island [two editions: 1972, 1989]
A Guide to Dorset Ghosts
Ghosts of Dorset, Devon and Somerset
with Mary Collier, Tom Perrott
Afterword, *Coker's Survey of Dorsetshire* [for the 1980 second edition of the 1732 work]
Editor *Steep Holm – a case history in the study of ecology*
Annotator *Monumenta Britannica* with John Fowles [first edition as two volumes 1980, 1982: volume one re-issued as an expanded first American edition, 1981]
Exploring Ancient Wiltshire with George Osborn
Old Portland with Jean M. Edwards
Romans in Britain
Purbeck Walks [three editions: 1983, 1985, 1988]
Old Swanage
The Dorset Walk with Ron Dacombe, Colin Graham
Stonehenge Antiquaries
Guide to Purbeck Coast and Shipwreck
Hardy Country Walks
The Steep Holm Guide
Lulworth and Tyneham Revisited
Walks in West Dorset
The Blandford Forum Guide
Dorset's War 1939-45
East Dorset Country Walks
Blackmore Vale and Cranborne Chase Walks
Exploring the Heartland of Purbeck
Brownsea – Dorset's Fantasy Island
Purbeck's Heath – nature, claypits and the oilfield
Wincanton's Directory [annually 1987-90]
Mysterious Dorset
Walks in Dorset's Hardy Country
National Trust Dorset with Colin Graham
Lawrence of Arabia in Dorset
Steep Holm Wildlife with Tony Parsons
Dorset Encyclopaedic Guide
Dorset at War – Diary of WW2
Literary Dorset

Contents

Introduction

CERNE ABBAS is one of the most compelling of Dorset villages because it has inherited a town-sized history. Unlike many other places in Dorset it also receives its fair share of attention and more. Visitors will always be drawn to explore these ancient streets by the even earlier and dominating absurdity of a full-frontal male nude sculpted into the nearby hillside.

Until the middle of the nineteenth century Cerne was still an important town. In 1836 engineers surveyed a railway line through the middle of Cerne, with a station replacing the Tithe Barn, but it was never built and the Bath to Weymouth route was eventually to take the Frome valley instead. Between 1851 and 1901 the population of Cerne Abbas was halved, from 1,200 to 586, and past authors have blamed this on the absence of the railway. This argument cannot, however, be sustained as the equivalent comparable downland town that received this railway, Maiden Newton, also suffered a major slump and like Cerne had a 600 population in 1901.

The present compilation is intended as a potted history of the visible relics of antiquity, monasticism and the town life that still litter Cerne. The ancient market town suffered only minor losses in the Demolishing Sixties and most of what's left found caring and moneyed owners in the Renovating Seventies. The place must not become a museum; it has more history than the average museum will ever accommodate.

1 **The Cerne Giant, on Giant Hill.**

1 **The Cerne Giant, in classic poses from the west; from the downs [above] and a layby on the valley road [below].**

THE ONE hundred and eighty foot high outline of a naked man, brandishing a one hundred and twenty foot club, overlooks the Cerne valley from the eastern escarpment, half-a-mile north of Cerne Abbas village in the downlands of central Dorset. It comprises a series of trenches, each two feet across, cut into the chalk of the hillside. These have been periodically scoured through the centuries to prevent the figure turning into a "green man" and eventually disappearing into the turf. This must have been the fate of the vast majority of colossal figures, as the neglect of one lifetime would be sufficient to cast such ecologically fragile art-forms to oblivion. It would be illogical to think that the Cerne Giant in Dorset, the Uffington White Horse in Oxfordshire, and the Long Man of Wilmington, Sussex, could represent the original total of ancient hill figures.

Despite supposition to the contrary, principally my own, in the 1970s, the recent evidence supports the traditional archaeological belief that the Cerne Giant is a depiction of the Roman god Hercules. The figure has the attributes of Hercules, though the one that clinches the matter is hidden below the grass. He is a native Celtic version of the god, portrayed naked just as he was in Gallo-Roman statuettes of the first century AD. The club is in his right hand and there was a lion's skin draped over his other arm.

This was rediscovered in the summer of 1979 by computer analysis of resistivity-meter readings taken across the general area below the Giant's left elbow [the right side as you look at him]. The survey was carried out by Yorkshire Television for their series of documentaries, "The Mysterious World". The original trench outlining the lion's skin survives beneath the grass as a pocket of softer and damper subsoil.

Features of the Giant's anatomy have also changed as a result of the succession of scourings. When a trench was in an overgrown or collapsed condition it was tempting to cut another beside it. This has shifted the lines of the figure's left leg, the left side of his body and the left arm – in fact the whole of the right side of the figure as you look at it from below. I found this from comparisons between aerial photographs. Those taken under dry conditions show the former trenches clearly, appearing as darker lines in the grass. The nose also survives in the ground, with long parallel sides joined with the eyes like an inverted phallus. It was common in Celtic art for the eyes and nose to be shown as an upside-down phallus. Though the nose has long been grassed over it can still be traced as a hump.

The Giant's penis now has a length of twenty-two feet but this is more of an exaggeration than the designers intended. Gerald Pitman of Sherborne was the first to notice that a scouring of the early twentieth century had absorbed the navel into its tip and thereby extended the

1 **Cerne Giant, left as he is and above with his cloak temporarily restored [in white paint] by Yorkshire Television.**

organ by six feet. The total length of the phallus, including the testicles, is now thirty feet.

Representations of the phallus were common in British Celtic culture and throughout the Roman world. Local examples include a Celtic head in the shape of a penis found at Eype, near Bridport, and a phallus riding a horse, incised on the lid of a third century water-jar from a pottery site at Linwood, near Ringwood. Phallic pendants in bronze were found during the rebuilding of London after the Great Fire, being described by John Aubrey as "little priapuses" in his *Monumenta Britannica*. Others, realistic rather than stylistic, exist in pottery. There were also oil lamps in the shape of a phallus. A south Italian wall painting depicts a huge phallus standing in the middle of the living room floor. Phallic representations were commonplace in the ancient world, much as crosses were in the middle ages, and they would have caused no offence or comment.

The place-name Cerne is relevant to this discussion of the Giant, as Cernunnos was a stag-headed Druidic deity reputedly larger than life. Cernunnos, according to the mediaeval Welsh *Mabinogion*, was a "lord of the wild beasts" who wielded an "iron club" and was "not smaller than two of the men of this world". The Celtic Gundestrup cauldron shows Cernunnos with a serpent in his left hand: if the Cerne 'cloak' trails off above the hand then it would be a snake! If a male nude can survive against all the odds on a Dorset hillside then it is no more bizarre to imagine him originally as part of a frieze of gods – a kind of hillside wallpaper – that have otherwise vanished into the grass.

In the low sun of January 1969 and again during the extreme drought of July 1976 I observed and recorded the outline of what seemed to be a dog, identical in shape to Roman bronze terriers found at Wroxeter and Carrawburgh, beginning about a hundred and fifteen feet from the Giant's right leg (the left one as you look at him). It has a length of about one hundred and fifty feet. Like the Giant, it is cut in full proportions, without any allowance for perspective or the foreshortening inherent in hill-art. Reduced to a horizontal plane both would be ten per-cent shorter.

At that time I concurred with Bernard C. Pickard who had written about a decorated skillet handle, depicting the Celtic god Nodons, that had been found on Hod Hill, near Blandford. He wrote in the *Illustrated London News* that it was "likely that the Cerne Giant can now join the Uffington White Horse as a purely British artform, untainted by any classical influences from the Romans." Pickard pointed out the shared attributes of the Cerne Giant – then still without a confirmed cloak – and the native god Nodons. I thought that the

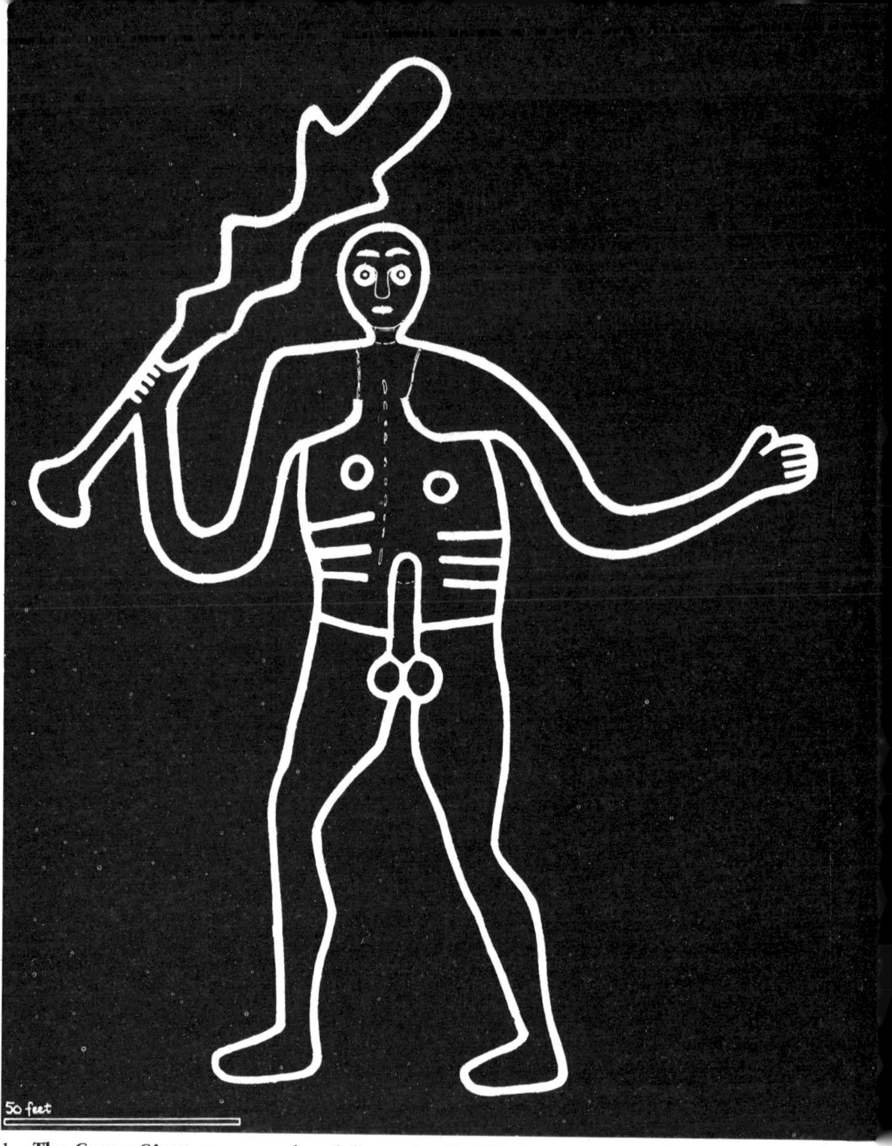

1 **The Cerne Giant, measured and drawn by Sir Flinders Petrie, 1926. If reduced to a horizontal plane, as on a map, the figure would be about ten per cent shorter. Opposite, drawn from oblique aerial shots, he appears tubbier.**

outline of the terrier could be considered as supporting evidence for this identification, as Mortimer Wheeler found votive representations of dogs, including one carved on a pot in which coins had been offered, during the excavation of a Romano-Celtic temple to Nodons at Lydney Park in the Forest of Dean. The lion's skin, however, conclusively demolishes the Nodons connection.

Not that it has any bearing upon the presence of a dog. Cernunnos,

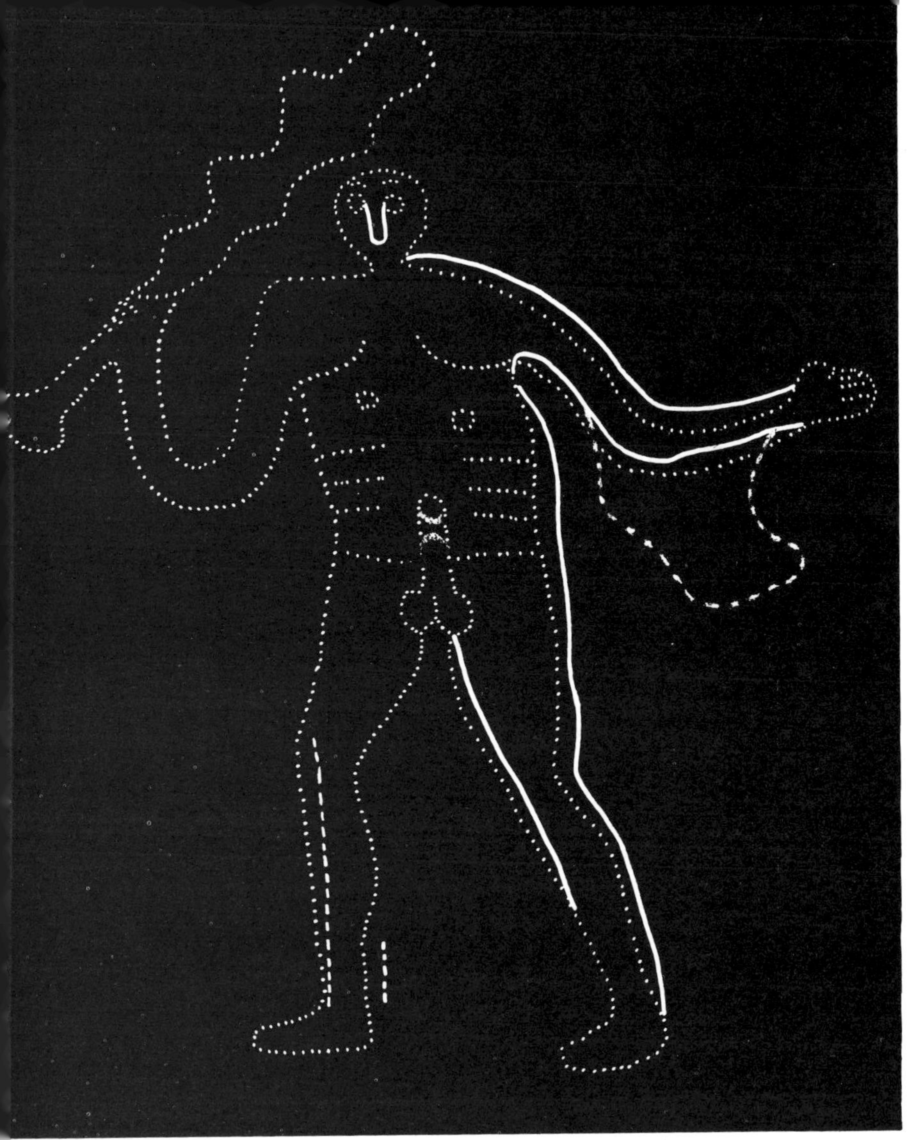

The Cerne Giant, drawn by Rodney Legg from aerial photographs, 1986. The present outline is shown by dots. Original trenches which are not grassed over are shown with a continuous line. Broken lines depict indistinct trenching of one leg and the cloak.

in a silver cauldron found at Gundestrup, Denmark, is shown surrounded by animals, though they are wild rather than domesticated. Hercules, too, had his infernal hound. As Heracles, one of the oldest heroes in Greek mythology, he had as his last and heaviest labours the ordeal of bringing the dog Cerberus up out of the underworld. This he did by strength of arm, carrying him to Eurystheus and back into Hades.

Hercules was worshipped far from the shrines of Attica. As the founder of the Olympian tradition he was the deity of the gymnasium and the feasts of Hercules were marked with athletic contests. In Rome he was coupled with the Muses and associated with hot baths, the wild olive and white poplar trees. He became fused with the deity Sancus or Dius Fidius, into the wide ranging master of happiness, industry, war and honour. He was also Hercules Saxarius, Hercules of the stone, and worshipped in the quarries. There is another outdoor outline of Hercules in Britain, cut into a Cumbrian rock-face. Cernunnos, however, would seem more appropriate than Hercules for Celtic worshippers.

The oldest name, apart from Cerne itself, that can be associated with the Giant is that of Helith, recorded in the thirteenth century. Walter de Hemingford, an Austin friar at Gisburn, Yorkshire, chronicled that Cerne was "in Dorsetensi pago... in quo pago olim colebantur deus Helith". Cerne, he wrote, was in the pagan district of Dorset where the god Helith was once worshipped. This is the earliest reference to Helith, which from field name evidence would appear to have been the mediaeval name of the Cerne Giant. Walter de Hemingford, the chronicler, is known also as Walter of Coventry. He completed his history in 1297.

The first direct written mention of the Cerne Giant did not take place for another five hundred years. Dr Richard Pococke, later bishop of Meath, visited Cerne in October 1754 and wrote in his *Travels through England* of "a figure cut in lines" that was "called the Giant and Hele, about 150 feet long, a naked figure in a genteel posture. It seems to be Hercules, or Strength and Fidelity, but it is with such indecent circumstances as to make one conclude it was also a Priapus. It is to be supposed that this was an ancient figure of worship, and one would imagine that the people would not permit the monks to destroy it."

Pococke also records that the outlines of the Giant were scoured every seven or eight years on the instructions of the lord of the manor.

William Stukeley also saw the Cerne Giant about this time and told the Society of Antiquaries of this "primitive Hercules" in 1764, giving him "the name of Helis". This he presumably acquired from the chroniclers via William Camden's *Britannia*, which had seized upon the god's name – without mention of the Giant – and said that at Cerne Augustine "had broken there in pieces Heil the Idol of the heathen English-Saxons".

In the twentieth century the task of keeping the Giant white became one of the National Trust's obligations, delegated in recent times to the firm of Beard and Company from Swindon. This used to be a communal chore and had the village and estate not kept the process going for centuries, right through the era of its Benedictine monastery, then the figure would have been lost. Many times it must have been a close-run thing as only one lethargic generation would have left the Giant obscured. He was in poor condition on the eve of the 1868 scouring, according to the Dorset County Chronicle: "This ancient and well-known colossal figure, which is carved on the declivity of the chalk hill overlooking the town, has for some years presented a shabby appearance on account of the trenches being choked with weeds and rubbish and the outlines being otherwise defaced. Orders have been given by Lord Rivers to have his 'Mightiness' cleaned and restored as near as possible to his original condition."

The Cerne Giant and a small parcel of land, delineated originally by a six-sided enclosure, was given to the National Trust by the Pitt-Rivers estate in 1920, having been withdrawn from sale as the village and surrounding farms were offered at public auction in 1919. Mr Senior, the auctioneer, announced that the "sculptured hill figure, an interesting object known all over England and also very possibly in the Colonies", would be reserved out of the sale together with the right of access to him.

In 1940 the Home Guard covered the Cerne Giant with brushwood to prevent him acting as a navigation aid for German bombers heading towards Bristol.

The viewing point for admiring the Giant is a layby on the A352, the Dorchester to Sherborne valley road, at the junction on the north side of the village [the 'A' designation of this valley road may be moved to the hill road across the downs at some future date]. You can also walk up to the Giant from here, by turning along the roads signposted "Village centre". In a hundred yards, after the milestone but before the school sign, there is a turning to the left. This lane bridges the Cerne River. The Giant's enclosure is up to the left from the end of the track.

There is a path to the Giant from the village, beginning at the end of Abbey Street. You turn right into the graveyard, under the stone arch and through the iron gate. Turn left across the centre of the cemetery to the wall facing you on the other side. Here there is a smaller arched gate, with a small cross and shield carved into one of the jambs. Walk into the field, where you pass to the rear of the mediaeval Gatehouse and cross the site of Cerne Abbey, proceeding diagonally to the opposite corner. There is a wooden stile beside the clump of beech trees. On the other side is a National Trust black-painted board about the Cerne Giant and behind this a path rises along the slope.

1a Fertility and the Giant.

IT WAS first recorded in 1893 that Cerne people believed that copulation whilst lying in the grass of the phallus of the Cerne Giant is a cure for barrenness in women. A more refined version, subdued for telespeak and guidebooks, is that girls have merely to sit on that part of the Giant if they wish to invoke the charm.

There is also the disputed evidence that the village's annual outbreak of revelry and youthful passion was also centred on a point close to the Giant. The maypole, it has been repeatedly stated, stood in the Trendle earthwork, a hundred feet above the figure. There is a definite record that Cerne's permanent maypole was removed in the puritanism of the seventeenth century (the churchwarden in 1635 "Paid Anthony Thorne and others for taking down ye maypole and make a town ladder of it") but this does not help with its location. The occasion was revived following the restoration of Charles II, with a temporary pole being erected each May Day.

Colley March, writing in 1901, quoted Mr Childs, an old sexton at Cerne, saying it was a fir-bole that was raised at night, being erected in the ring just above the Giant: "It was decorated, and the villagers went up and danced round the pole on the first of May. Nothing of the sort is now done." Others, writing from 1925 to 1939, describe this in terms that amount to "fake-lore" rather than folklore. Villagers have pointed out that the Trendle or Frying Pan earthwork contained the stumps of a small fir plantation, and said that the maypole was erected in the village, being set into the green by theTown Pond towards the north end of Abbey Street.

2 The Trendle or Frying Pan.

THE TRENDLE, or Frying Pan as it is known in Cerne, is an ancient earthwork enclosure on Giant Hill, a hundred and fifty feet above the Giant's outstretched arm. It is double banked, with both banks squarish on the north and east sides, and rounded corners towards the north-west and north-east, bending into a general curve for the other two corners. The north side is a hundred and twenty feet long, and the west side about a hundred feet. The outer bank is original but the inner ditch and bank may have been dug about 1825, to surround a small planting of fir trees.

But the Trendle would not have been constructed originally to fence a clump of trees. It you study the photographs on page 8 and opposite, you will see that it has been cut as a terrace into the hillside. At the far left corner, the north-east, its builders have created a distinct

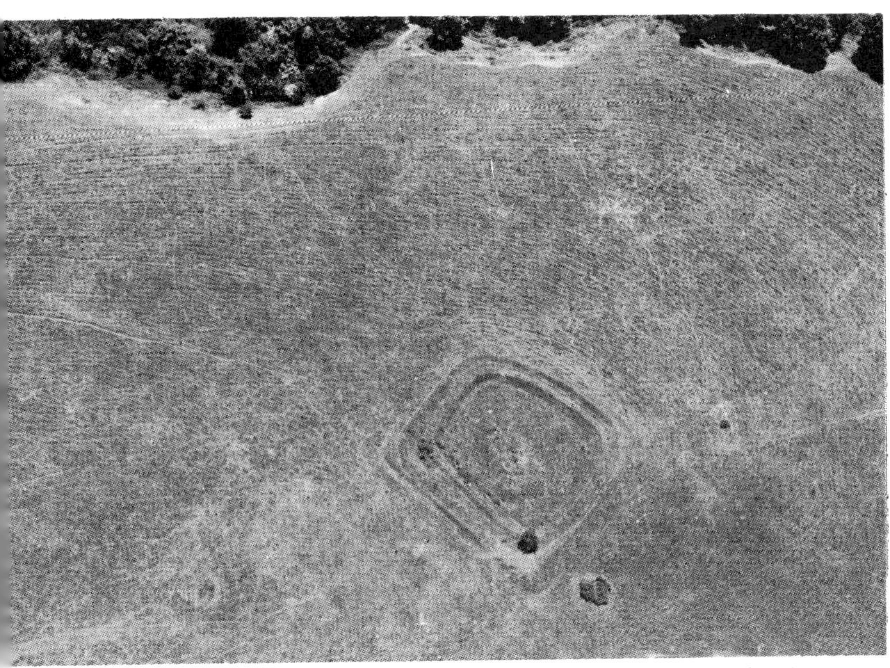

2 **The Trendle earthwork, seen from the air. It is visible as a terrace in the pictures on page 8 [above the Giant's outstretched left arm].**

cutting, and conversely the opposite corner, the south-west, is embanked.

This was done to provide a flat platform for a building or some ceremonial purposes, rather than to hold stock or fence trees. Digging into the hillside would have been a needless task for a stock pen, and a senseless one for young trees as none would have grown in the exposed chalk bedrock of the northern half of the earthwork. Logically, there would have been an entrance but this was presumably blocked at the time of the tree planting.

It is tempting to suppose that it might have enclosed the platform on which a Roman temple was built – a temple to Hercules would be an antiquary's dream – but examination of molehills and rumoured illegal searchings by metal detectors revealed none of the debris that could be expected to litter such a site. A first century Romano-Celtic temple, however, would have been of totally timber construction, unlike the flint and mortar foundations of later buildings. The issue must be regarded as open until tested by excavation. For what it is worth, the relationship between the Giant and Trendle is that the south side of his body is in a direct line with the north side of the earthwork.

3 **Stone kerbing around the well at the site of St Augustine's Chapel.**

3 St Augustine's Well, in the churchyard, Abbey Street.

A SPRING wells up in a depression sheltered by trees at the centre of the cemetery, formerly the Abbey churchyard, at the end of Abbey Street. It has a kerbing of stones and is known as St Augustine's Well. Thomas Gerard, writing in his *Survey of Dorsetshire* in the 1620s (reprinted 1982 by Dorset Publishing Co) says that it was "heretofore covered with a Chappell dedicated to St Augustine".

Gerard recorded an old tradition that Cerne was "soe named from the Words of St Augustine, who, when he preached Christianity to the Inhabitants of these Partes, pitched downe his Staffe on the Grounde, using these Wordes (*Cerne quid hic sit*), whence immediatelie flowed a quick Fountaine, that served to baptize manie, whom, with this Miracle as well as his Doctrine, hee had converted."

John Leland, Henry VIII's antiquary, wrote that Edwold (brother of Edmund the king of East Anglia martyred in 871) had lived as a hermit near "the silver well", this "fountain" of St Augustine at Cerne. The relics of Edwold were transferred from a shrine at the Abbey to "the old church at Cerne, where now is the parish church."

Augustine (not to be confused with the earlier Augustine of Hippo) was sent to England as a missionary, with forty monks, by Pope Gregory I, in 596. He founded the monastery of Christ Church, Canterbury, and was consecrated bishop of the English in 597 and first archbishop of Canterbury in 601. He died in 604.

The St Augustine connection with Cerne is firmly documented in mediaeval manuscripts. Gotselin, writing in the eleventh century and put into English by Jerome Porter in 1632, says that the "demoniac" inhabitants of a heathen village in the province of Dorsaeta tied fishes' tails to the rumps of Augustine and his monks and drove them away. When the party rested to recover from this, Augustine struck his staff on the ground and a fountain issued, the chronicler saying he had seen this well and a chapel built over it.

William of Malmesbury, writing in the twelfth century, says that Augustine came westwards to Dorset after converting Kent, and retreated three miles to Cerne after the fish-tail incident. He gives Cernel as the location of the miraculous spring and says that Augustine gave it this name, from the Latin Cerno ("I see") and Hel which he, wrongly unfortunately, states "is the Hebrew for God".

By 1483 Caxton had translated Jacobus de Voragine's *Golden Legend* and in it the above events are ascribed to "a certain town inhabited by wicked people" though there is the delightful embellishment, sustained by Cerne legend into the eighteenth century, that those who had driven out Augustine had all their children born with tails, until they repented. F. J. Harvey Darton, who collected the variants of these stories in his *English Fabric*, gives another Kent connection – the kingdom of Kent being where Augustine went first to baptise Ethelbert – in mentioning the similar stories about the Kentish "long-tails".

An entry of 1761 in the Cerne churchwardens' accounts gives another name to this holy well – "Paid John Thorne's Bill for work about Saint Paston's well. £1. 5s. 0d."

4 Abbey Church, Abbey Street.

THE NINTH century monastery of Cerne was reformed and refounded on Benedictine lines by Ethelmaer, Earl of Cornwall, towards the end of the century. The buildings were completed in about 987, the time of King Edgar, and had the author Aelfric, who would become known as Grammaticus, as their first Abbot. Eleven of his influential treatises survive in print. Cerne, meanwhile, was raided by Canute, who later made full recompense after he had been crowned King of all England in 1017.

These buildings were rebuilt in the twelfth century and suffered complete destruction after the dissolution of the larger monastic

4 **The field that was once an Abbey, between the churchyard and Giant Hill.**

houses by Henry VIII in 1539.

Thomas Corton, the last Abbot, was accused of a catalogue of offences and indiscretions by the High Commissioner who investigated the management of the religious houses. Parts of his account, published in the *Victoria County History* are of *Sun* quality, including the revelation that he "mated with his concubines" – although he was decent enough to do this off the precincts, in his cellarer's house. The "goods of the monastery" were wasted upon them, and his children. The monks also enjoyed a liberal regime, being spared the tedium of masses and allowed to "play at dice all night".

The Abbey Church, the heart of the monastery, and its conventual buildings stood in what is now the eastern half of the cemetery at the end of Abbey Street and across the centre of the field beneath the nearest spur of Giant Hill.

There is a public path across the monastic field, from the gateway in the cemetery wall. A stone, unearthed in 1986, is carved with a cherub and inscribed: "This Wall was Erected in 1838." It has been re-erected above the gate. The Abbey stood on the other side. Although there is now little or nothing to see it is a tranquil and sheltered spot beneath the hill and its trees. A little more was visible until the nineteenth century. Dr Richard Pococke observed the remains of "three or four ruins which seem to have been of round towers".

Apart from that nothing is known of their design or extent, beyond the humps and hollows in the field. Green-glazed mediaeval pottery turns up in the molehills there and mediaeval pottery slip-tiles, with stylised foliage and shields, have been dug up in the further parts of the cemetery. Two of these, from the supposed site of the Lady Chapel, were given me in 1976 by Arthur Stride, whose brother was the Cerne land agent for the Pitt-Rivers estate before 1914.

One has a petal pattern and the other the arms of Clare, dating from the end of the thirteenth century or first years of the fourteenth. Laurence Keen, the county archaeologist, drew my attention to identical designs at Sherborne Abbey and the Old Castle in Sherborne and suggested they had been made by the mediaeval pottery at Hermitage, excavated in 1959, which lies between the two abbeys.

Cerne was a major religious house with substantial lands in Dorset and a cell on Brownsea Island in Poole Harbour. The abbot of "Cerneli" is listed many times in the ownership census of Domesday Book. Some pews with richly carved ends were moved down the street from the Abbey after the Dissolution, into the parish church, and are said to have been removed to the Blackmore Vale parish of Hilfield in 1860 though Dorset's ecclesiastical historian, F. P. Pitfield, says that by then the Hilfield benches had long been in place.

4 **Monastic tiles from the site of the Abbey Church at Cerne Abbas, featuring a floral design and the arms of Clare [right].They were given to the author by Arthur Stride.**

4 | **Arguably from Cerne Abbey – a bench-end at Hilfield church [Ordnance Survey map reference ST 635 051].**

4a The Book of Cerne, now at Cambridge University.

THE *Book of Cerne*, a monastic manuscript principally of the Passion and Resurrection, was one of the possessions of Cerne Abbey, though it is unlikely to have been written here. It was originally the book of Aethelwold, the bishop of Lichfield in the early ninth century, or perhaps even Aethelwold of Lindisfarne a century earlier. A later appendix contains the *Charters of Cerne Abbey* plus prayers, which touch upon the separateness of a monk's life from the world, and "all kinds of sins which the Devil brings to lead to uncleanness: sodomy, fornication natural and unnatural, masturbation with male and female". The *Book of Cerne* was given to Cambridge University by George I in 1715.

5 **The Porch to the Abbot's Hall, engraved for 'The Beauties of England and Wales' in 1803.**

GATE HOUS

5 The Porch to the Abbot's Hall, though it is wrongly called the 'Gate House' – a misnomer which unfortunately stuck – drawn by John Cary for the best illustrated and by far the rarest edition of John Hutchins's 'County History' of Dorset, the second edition of 1796-1815. Note, in the background, that the Cerne Giant is delineated sans genitalia.

5 **The Porch to the Abbot's Hall, seen from the south-west approaches [opposite] with its splendid window [above].**

5 **Porch, rear [east] view from the Abbot's Hall site.**

5 Porch to Abbot's Hall, Abbey Street.

THE PORCH to the Abbot's Hall is the finest piece of architecture in Cerne Abbas, surviving in the grounds of Abbey Farm where it fronts the lawn and backs on to the pasture that covers the site of the Abbot's Hall and Abbey Church. It was built by Abbot Thomas Sam (1497-1509), apparently in 1508.

Three storeys in height, the yellow-brown Ham-stone building is embellished with a wealth of heraldic carvings, including a Tudor rose and a string of shields-of-arms with those of the Duchy of Cornwall, France and England, the Abbey and Abbot Thomas himself. Family shields identify various patrons such as Fitz-James, Latimer, Newburgh, Wadham, Uvedale, Martin of Athelhampton, and Hugh Oldham (the bishop of Exeter).

The door opens into the porch with its fan-vaulted roof. Adjoining the north side of the porch is the two storey porter's lodge. Both parts were derelict by 1840 and were then attractively restored. The large mediaeval leaded window is comparable with that at Forde Abbey.

The Porch is often called the "Gatehouse" – which it was not. This incompetence extends to the Ordnance Survey. The remains of the South Gate are inside Abbey Farm. The other gatehouse was at the North Gate, south-west of the Giant near Kettle Bridge.

6 Abbey Farm, formerly South Gatehouse, Abbey Street.

ABBEY FARM, the manor-type mansion at the north end of Abbey Street, incorporates monastic walls at its north-east and southern sides and a Saxon doorway discovered during building work in the 1950s. This is the earliest surviving fragment of Abbey stonework at Cerne.

Part of the main arch of the South Gate was also found, with the remains of a pintle on which one of its great hinges rested. This was torn down by rioters in the sixteenth century, in the reign of Edward VI, when two hundred men "tore down the hedges about Cerne and did breake or shake in pieces the South Gate". There is a contemporary account that "convenyent high-waies" fanned out from this point, though it is now a cul-de-sac.

Much other Abbey stonework is reset into the Abbey Farm, from the main buildings which had been "raised" about 1580. The principal reconstruction and enlargement of Abbey Farm took place after 1641 when it came into the ownership of Denzil Holles through his marriage to Jane Freke, a widow.

6 **Abbey Farm was the South Gatehouse to the Abbey.**

Denzil Holles had leapt to fame with an incident in Parliament. As the member for Dorchester he restrained the Speaker to his chair and prevented the adjournment of a debate on religious innovation and taxation, with the words: "God's wounds. You shall sit till we please to rise."

Holles died in 1679 and is buried at St Peter's church in Dorchester. The house was restored between 1951-55.

7 Abbey Guest-house, Abbey Street.

THE STONE-ROOFED building behind Abbey Farm, with its fine oriel window, was erected during the time of John Vanne, abbot from 1458-70, and appears to have been used as a guest-house. It may, however, have been built as the abbot's lodging. Vanne's initials are carved on its fireplace, which has since been reset in the Abbey Farm. The building formerly extended further east, towards the main monastic buildings which have now completely disappeared.

7 **Opposite. Stone slates stripped from the abbey Guest-house during its restoration. The oriel window is on the upper storey [centre right].**

7 **Abbey Guest-house seen before restoration [above and opposite] with the quaintness of the oriel window enhanced by a roof-top fern garden which would have delighted the Victorians.**

The most romantic figure from English history to have been dined in the Abbey's hospitality suite was Margaret of Anjou [1430-82], queen consort of Henry VI. She had landed at Weymouth, from France, on 14 April 1471 and went the following day to Cerne Abbey to rendezvous with her supporters, led by the Duke of Somerset and the Earl of Devonshire. She was "right heavy and sore" at hearing that whilst she was disembarking at Weymouth, on that fateful Easter Sunday, the Lancastrian cause had fallen on the battlefield at Barnet with death for Warwick and captivity for Henry. Edward IV had carried the Yorkists to victory in the War of the Roses.

8 **Barton Farm was the Abbey's Tithe Barn.**

8 The Tithe Barn, now Barton Farm.

BUILT IN stone with masses of squared flints, in about 1350, the monastic Tithe Barn at Cerne stands at the opposite end of the village from the Abbey. It is to the south of The Folly, the road leading up to Acreman Street.

Its present length is a hundred and thirty feet but this is not excessive for the tithe barn of a major abbey and it used to be much longer – extending northwards half way to The Folly.

The surviving length of barn was partly converted into a farmhouse, called Barton Farm, in the eighteenth century. By 1886 the remaining barn part was derelict and collapsing, being saved and rebuilt on the command of its owner, Lieutenant General Augustus Pitt-Rivers, the father of archaeology. But he was totally committed to excavations on Cranborne Chase and delegated his Cerne responsibilities, the barn instructions being trimmed to avoid the demanding task of copying all the original woodwork. Only the rafters above the impressive porches preserve the genuine roof design.

9 Abbey Mill, Silley Court.

THE TRACES of the former Abbey Mill, just a couple of buttresses, are on the east bank of the Cerne River, which used to be known as the River Silley, downstream from the Kettle Bridge. A sluice still trickles into the river two hundred feet downstream from the bridge. There are also the banks of its former leat, which provided the head of water into a top-shoot wheel which would have been set in a chamber beneath ground level. All this lies on the bank opposite the Millbank public footpath and is not accessible for exploration.

10 Silley Court Barn, Silley Court.

THE BARN at the north end of the yards behind Abbey Farm, near the bend in the lane east of Kettle Bridge is dated by the Royal Commission on Historical Monuments to the fifteenth century "probably" but its porches are modern. This area, known as Silley Court, was one of the working areas of the monastic establishment. The upper reaches of the Cerne River were known as the River Silley, and this barn held the grain for the Abbey Mill.

10 **The barn for the Abbey Mill, at Silley Court.**

11 **Kettle Bridge, across the Cerne River upstream from the former Abbey Mill.**

11 Kettle Bridge, Millbank.

KETTLE BRIDGE, a single stone and flint span across the Cerne River at the north end of the Millbank footpath, south-west of the Giant, carried the cart traffic to the Abbey's North Gate. The present structure could date from the monastic period as the Royal Commission on Historical Monuments say it is seventeenth century "or earlier" but either way it would have had a predecessor.

12 Beaver Field, Alton Lane.

THE FIELD east of the Abbey site, on the left of Alton Lane – locally this was known as Blood-and-Guts Lane – opposite the last buildings as you ascend towards the Old Sherborne Road, is known as "Beaver", "Bever" or "Bee-vor". This derives from its mediaeval name of "Belle Voir" or "Boire", meaning a pleasuance of garden walks.

13 Cat-and-Chapel, now New Barn, Piddle Lane.

THE MONKS of Cerne Abbey erected a beacon chapel on the seven hundred and fifty foot summit of Black Hill, the promontory south-east of the village. It was dedicated to St Catherine, the patron saint of spinsters, and the site, of which nothing remained, was known as Cat-and-Chapel, "Cat-and" being the local garbled form of Catherine.

This is now the yard of the New Barn, in the middle of the high open ground at the top of Piddle Lane, opposite the Ordnance Survey's triangulation pillar.

14 Cerne Park, west of village.

CERNE'S MEDIAEVAL deer park, owned by the Abbey, lies across one hundred and five acres of wooded coombes to the west of the village, south-east from the television relay mast. The pale of Cerne Park still

14 **Woods and fields within the pale of Cerne Park.**

largely survives, as a five-foot high bank supporting dense hedges.

A public footpath crosses the area, leaving the hill-top ridgeway that overlooks the Sydling valley immediately on the northern side of the television mast compound. You then follow the right-hand hedgerow of the field for a hundred and fifty yards. A grassy path then goes through the hedge and into a hazel coppice. The track descends into the bowl of the valley for a quarter of a mile, to a stile that brings you out of the wood into the floor of the coombe. Roe deer, wild and free these days, are common.

15 **St Mary's, the parish church, at noon. Giant Hill is beyond, with the Trendle earthwork on the skyline towards the right. Opposite, the tower is seen from the Old Market House at the south end of Abbey Street.**

15 Parish Church of St Mary, Abbey Street.

THE PARISH church of St Mary, on the east side of Abbey Street, has surviving walls and windows from a small church of the thirteenth century. F. P. Pitfield, writing in *Dorset Parish Churches* (Dorset Publishing Co), considers the church originated late in the thirteenth century. But my reference on page 16, to Edwold's relics being transferred to "the old church at Cerne, where now is the parish church", suggests there was an earlier building on the site.

The present impressive structure with its tall gargoyled tower dates

The Old Market House
The Old Market House

from the early sixteenth century, before the closure of the Abbey, when the building was extended forwards to the street. Minor changes followed in the seventeenth century, which provided the fine oak pulpit and a now disused communion table, as well as the painted wall texts which were resurrected from the later limewash in 1961. Roofs were renewed in extensive renovations from then until 1967 and the stonework was cleaned. Victorian box-pews were replaced with rush-bottomed chairs, such were the transient whims of the swinging nineteen-sixties.

The former treasure in Cerne church was its previous pewing, removed and sold for a hundred guineas in 1860. These had elaborately carved ends and had almost certainly come from the Abbey. Whether they survived is doubtful; Mr Pitfield refutes a village story that they went to Hilfield, a tiny church in the Blackmore Vale.

16 Market or Preaching Cross, in churchyard, Abbey Street.

THE EARLY 15th century cross that stands in the middle of the parish cemetery, at the end of Abbey Street, has been identified as a preaching cross but it may well be the remains of the town's market cross. Alfred Pope, writing in 1906, pointed out that a town of Cerne's former status would have had a market cross. Whichever type it is, the bits have almost certainly been moved from another site as the cross would normally have been mounted on steps. These are missing, and nearby grave digging has shown that nothing is hidden beneath the ground.

What survives is a massive octagonal Ham stone socket, chamfered around its top edge, with each side eighteen inches across. Set into the centre is the first stage of the cross shaft, fifteen inches in diameter at the base and 2 ft. 3 ins. high.

17 Congregational Chapel, Abbey Street.

THE CONGREGATIONAL Chapel in Abbey Street was built in 1888 and has a schoolroom at the rear. An adjoining schoolroom, built in 1863,had burnt down and the £67 insurance payment went a large way to paying General Augustus Pitt-Rivers £100 for the chapel site. The new building replaced a chapel that had been enlarged and renovated in 1820. An earlier meeting house was on the north side and when it was partially demolished a century ago the stripping of plaster revealed wall texts: "O give thanks unto the Lord."

17 **Typical late Victorian brick facade of the Congregational Chapel.**

James Troubridge, pastor for 51 years in the nineteenth century, described Cerne as it was when he arrived in 1812: "Darkness covered the place, and gross darkness the people. Vice and immorality abounded on every hand. The Sabbath was universally profaned, being used for pleasure, business, and getting drunk." Times, perhaps, are not that changed.

18 The Lock-up, Long Street.

THE VILLAGE lock-up stands behind the flint wall opposite the Royal Oak Inn, on the south side of Long Street. It housed prisoners until the Police Station was built next to the New Inn.

19 The Stocks, Abbey Street.

THESE ARE now outside the parish church but were previously opposite the Town Pond in Abbey Street, and originally stood at Goose Green on the east side of Folly Bridge, at the end of Long Street. Folly Bridge used to bc known as Pain's Bridge, and the telephone box on the site of the stocks at Goose Green erroneously gives its location as "Swan Green", such are the pitfalls of place-names for the local historian. Wooden stocks were used for the restraint and humiliation of delinquents in the category of minor offences that could be dealt with summarily without recourse to the county gaol and assizes.

There were other fixtures for punishment at Cerne, the "cucking stool" for dipping females in the pond being constructed by Anthony Dracon from George Randall's timber in 1683. On 29 March 1685 the same Mr Dracon was paid four shillings for two days and a half in making the pillory. It required seven feet of oak and eight feet of ash board, the wood costing 6 s. 9 d.

Nineteenth century brickwork separated by an alleyway from the seventeenth century banded flint and chalk-clunch blocks of the thatched Bell Inn in Long Street – now the Old Bell tea-rooms.

20 Police Station and Court.

NEXT TO the New Inn in Long Street is the former Police Station and Court House. It is a flinty Victorian building, the petty sessions being held there for the first time on 30 May 1860. Previously they had been held next door in the New Inn.

The history of this beat is in the log-books of Pc Hebditch and Pc James Searley, which are now in the County Record Office. They are a catalogue of poaching, drunkenness, highway offences, theft and fire; with reminders that this was a different age. On 24 May 1892, Searley "birched a lad at Cerne by order of the magistrates".

21 The Workhouse, Sherborne Road.

THE AUSTERE Poor Law Union District Workhouse, built in 1836, stands at the north end of the village, where the down and out of the area had a prime view of the Giant. It is the big building overlooking the Sherborne Road.

At the end of the First World War the Workhouse saw the death from pneumonia of one of the last reddle-women – hawkers of sheep dies – eighty-year-old Mary Ann Bull whose cart was sold to pay for the funeral. Another unfortunate inmate, number 1299, seventy-nine-year-old Johnny Trott, died one morning in 1924 when he pulled the bell for breakfast and it came off the wall and landed on his head.

The Workhouse closed in 1930 and the substantial building became a youth hostel, at the height of the movement's popularity during the years of mass cycling and back-packing, but this too had its day and it is now a residential nursing home.

22 National School, Duck Street.

THE PRIMARY school in Duck Street opened in 1870 as a National School, under the auspices of the Anglican educational movement [the National Society for Promoting the Education of the Poor in the Principles of the Established Church] which had been established in 1811. The playground was provided later, after the thatched building on its site, the Prince of Wales inn, caught fire in an early winter snowstorm in November 1911. It was previously the Calcraft Arms but the landlady changed the name about 1860 when a Calcraft gained notoriety as the public hangman.

21 Opposite. The Giant's view of Giant View, the 1836 Union Workhouse. Beyond, above the woods of Cerne Park, is a television signal-booster mast.

23 **The New Inn was the main coaching inn when the village was a market town.**

23 New Inn.

STONEWORK THAT is intricately carved, probably from the high altar at the Abbey, is built into the wall at the east side of the New Inn. This was the village's coaching inn and its present structure dates from the eighteenth century, 1774 being the date on a lead pump. Until 1860 the New Inn was used as the village court house, A. O. Gibbons writes in his 1962 book *Cerne Abbas*. Magistrates held a monthly petty sessions:

"They sat in the room which is now the main bar of the inn, seated to the left of the fireplace, the prisoner being held in the present ladies' toilet until the hearing of the case. The decoratively twisted iron bars of this cell are still in position although boarded over."

The New Inn held bad memories for old Cerne villagers in the mid-twentieth century. It was to there that they were summoned by a church bell on the Saints' days at the quarters of the year to pay their rents to the land-agent for the Pitt-Rivers estate, Charles R. Stride. A threepenny beer voucher was given to each tenant as he paid. Though the estate was not sold-up until 1919 the paying of rents in the inn had to be abandoned in 1914 under the Defence of the Realm Act which restricted drinking hours.

24 Red Lion.

THIS IS the red-brick building on the south side of Long Street. It was built in 1898 and is typical late Victoriana, though there had been a beer-house on the site for centuries. Admire the fine early fireplace.

25 **The Royal Oak, built in the 1540s, incorporates carved stonework from demolitions at the Abbey which had been dissolved by Henry VIII.**

25 Royal Oak.

THERE IS some superb stonework in the Royal Oak Inn, at the narrows in Long Street; riches explicable only as its building in the early 1540s coincided with the first flush of demolitions at the abandoned Abbey. There are moulded beams, an original doorway at the side entrance to the upstairs, and a fine fireplace with a four-centred head.

The original part of the building is the section at the corner, in line with Abbey Street, and it was extended in the coaching era to incorporate stables, a forge and yard. The name Royal Oak is of late seventeenth century origin, celebrating Charles II's evasion of capture by hiding in an oak tree.

26 Elephant and Castle [now a guest house].

THE ELEPHANT AND CASTLE, a nineteenth century building in Duck Street, was delicensed in the 1970s. Its name was apparently derivative from the Infanta of Castile story though the 1930s sign, since abandoned, took some liberties. It became the "Sound of Water" guest house.

27. **Above and opposite. The finest range of Tudor houses in Dorset.**

27 Tudor Houses, Abbey Street.

THE ROW of Tudor Houses in Abbey Street – which gave it the caption "Street of Yesterday" in a 1950s postcard – dates from 1500 and was probably built by the Abbey for the use of its secular officials. It is built of stone with elaborate timber framing and an upper storey that overhangs the pavement; a building style typical of the south-eastern counties but unusual in Dorset. Thc bay window is an eighteenth century embellishment. Numbers one and two at the north end of the row are now one house, Barnwells. Number two used to be the Nag's Head Inn.

The doorway of number four, the Pitchmarket, has a carved wooden moulded head, in a double curve with blind tracery featuring two quatrefoils and flowers. This house is of special interest to Americans, being the most photogenic of the block with the bonus that it was the home of Thomas Washington, uncle of the first president. The initials of Thomas and his wife Maria (married 1676), "T.M.W.", were on a lead pump-head in an adjoining passage, but this piece of village history was sold to the Vidler family of Dorchester.

28 Acreman Street.

THE NAME means "Farm-worker" and there are streets with similar names in Dorchester and Sherborne. A reminder of this era is the range of ten labourers' tenements that runs along the east side of the street. They are of various dates and construction, from the seventeenth century at the north to 1832 near the other end of the line. One has a monastic head reset above its front door. A pair of seventeenth century cottages, now one house, stand on the other side of the road, near the Sydling turning, and have a 1727 extension.

This crossroads was widened and straightened in a road scheme in 1960, before which the former Greyhound Inn stood in a triangular plot in the fork of Hook's Corner. Its site is now The Folly junction. The road-works also opened up the formerly narrow north end of Acreman Street which had previously met the Sherborne road at a junction, to the south of the 1836 workhouse. The Sherborne Road then merged directly into Duck Street. Improving Acreman Street gave the village a by-pass but it also opened up a rustic backwater.

The Old Malthouse, number 14 Acreman Street, was until 1928 the Union Arms beer-house, taking its name from the Union Workhouse further up the valley. A. O. Gibbons records W. H. Gale and his brother watching a dancing bear outside the Union Arms; and the Jewish owner of a little shop on the opposite side of the road, whose religion enabled him to open for the sale of sweets on a Sunday.

28 **Monastic head, re-used on the front wall of a terraced cottage midway along the east side of Acreman Street. Initials and the date of the housebuilding, 1858, are carved below.**

29 **Andrews' Lane (below) leads to a footbridge across the Cerne River.**

29 Andrews' Lane.

FROM THE west side of Abbey Street, fifty yards before you reach Abbey Farm, Andrews' Lane branches off to the Cerne River. On the south side of the corner is Andrews' House, an early eighteenth century building that was the home of Samuel Andrews. The cobbled way, paved with up-edged pib stones, ran beside the wall that separated the Abbey's grounds and fishponds from the town.

30 Wills Lane.

WILLS LANE curves between Duck Street and Acreman Street. In the middle, on the knoll at Barton Lodge, are the trees of Cerne's large rookery.

32 **The Forge is on the north side of Mill Lane.**

31 Beach's Academy of Learning, Mill Lane.

DR WILLIAM BEACH'S Academy of Learning, with schoolrooms and dormitories, has a 1793 date-stone next to the Forge Cottage in Mill Lane. It functioned as a school until about 1860. George Squibb recalled hearing that the boys' and girls' dormitories were lighted by a single candle in a lantern set into a hole in the wall that separated them.

32 The Forge, Mill Lane.

THE FORGE in Mill Lane was established by Charles Curtis in the 1860s, probably in part of the school playground of the former Academy of Learning next door.

33 **Miller's Brook was General Booth's citadel in 'Darkest Cerne'.**

33 Salvation Army Citadel, Mill Lane.

THE MILLER'S BROOK in Mill Lane was a Salvation Army Citadel, operating in the late Victorian era but failing to last much longer than the queen's reign. It then became a store and chicken house before conversion to a restaurant.

34 The Mill, Mill Lane.

THE CORN crushing mill at the end of Mill Lane operated until 1933, when William Holland was the last miller.

35 The Old Saddler, Duck Street.

THE OLD SADDLER is the tall Georgian building on thc corner of Duck Street with the Folly. Though it went through changes in the nineteenth century it retains a shop front that is basically of 1800, neatly rounded with a central doorway set at an angle to the street. This has moulded woodwork with reeded pilasters at the side.

36 Former Tucking Mill, Up Cerne Lane.

FOUR HUNDRED yards along the lane towards Up Cerne, on the side of the stream, stood the Tucking Mill. Cloth was tented between rollers and hooks – "put on tenterhooks" as Cerne's historian A. O. Gibbons writes in his 1962 book.

37 Holly Bank, formerly The Glove, Sherborne Road.

THE COTTAGE on the east side of the Sherborne Road at the north end of the parish, beyond the turning to Up Cerne, used to be The Glove public house. Glove making was a traditional north Dorset industry, and survives in south Somerset. Cerne's Glove Factory was in the dip on the north side of the stream, immediately east of the Sherborne Road. It was demolished early in the twentieth century. Between the factory and its pub there is a track, running eastwards to the hill, which preserves the memory of another lost industry – Brick Kiln Drove.

38 The Giant's Head, Old Sherborne Road.

THE GIANT'S HEAD building stands on the east side of Old Sherborne Road – as this former turnpiked ridgeway is known to the traffic police, though locals call it The Top Road – at the northern extremity of Cerne parish. It is an isolated building a mile-and-a-half out of the village. This used to be a public house, but was closed down by the court following the Great War because of regular after-hours drinking.

39 The Old Bell, Long Street.

IT IS appropriate to round this guide off with another former alehouse, the thatched Bell Inn, as it has become the Old Bell tea-rooms. In the middle of Long Street, on the south side, it is also the notable Cerne example of distinctive chalkland architecture. The seventeenth century walls are neatly banded with layers of chalk-clunch blocks alternating with knapped flints. The inside retains original beams and such once vital apertures as the bread-oven and inglenook fireplace.

The last half hour of a civilised visitor's Cerne experience should be reserved for a Dorset clotted cream tea.

CERNE ABBAS is reasonably well covered in Dorset books, and is the subject of the following titles:

Baal Durotrigensis, Richard Sydenham, 1840. Concerns itself with the origins of the Cerne Giant, deviating into a wealth of bizarre theories.

English Fabric, F. Harvey Darton, 1936. The village that provides the core material for this study of country life is Cerne Abbas, and fragments of useful information are scattered amongst ponderous rural philosophy.

Cerne Abbas, Mary D. Jones, 1952. Much about the Abbey but less on the village itself.

Cerne Abbas, A. O. Gibbons, 1962. The fullest account of Cerne's village and trades, with reference to churchwardens' account books, business directories and other documentary sources being aided by colourful anecdotes.

Dorset and Cerne's God of the Celts, Dorset County Magazine special issue, number 66, by Rodney Legg, 1978. Speculation that Cerne's naked god might be Nodons, rather than Hercules, with claims for drought-lines showing an accompanying terrier.

The present writer has enjoyed compiling this summary of Cerne's visible history and would be pleased to hear from villagers with additional memories or information about their homes. Much must be locked in the vaults; property title deeds that building societies, banks and solicitors salt away. If you ever have the opportunity to look through yours, you may well learn a lot about your home, irrespective of its age as the deeds of modern houses often include copies of conveyances relating to the original estate from which the land was detached.

Muscovy duck beside the Town Pond, Abbey Street.

Parking in Cerne Abbas

On-street parking in Cerne Abbas becomes increasingly fraught as its popularity and population increase. Alternatively, visitors can leave their cars in the layby beside the main road, facing the Cerne Giant and the northern approach to the village.

Better still, you can turn from there into Duck Street and then left again in a hundred yards, on to an unclassified public road. Fifty yards down this lane, on the left, you come to the Kettle Bridge Picnic Site (Ordnance Survey map reference ST 664 015) which was opened by Hedley Hayward for West Dorset District Council in 1986.

From here you walk down to the bridge and turn right along Cerne Abbas footpath 1, which follows the riverbank and leads into the village.

In 200 yards it forks, with the left option becoming Andrews' Lane and leading to Abbey Street. The other path, Cerne Abbas footpath 31, continues downstream and becomes Mill Lane. It enters Duck Street near its junction with Long Street.

Both these paths are exceedingly pleasant and worth walking in their own right, irrespective of where you managed to leave your car. Back street Cerne abounds with ancient nooks and crannies and glimpses across delightful gardens. Here you can be almost alone, even on days when there are crowds in the three main streets.

CERNE WALKS

Walk 1. Seven mile northern circuit, extending to Minterne Parva and Up Cerne.

Start from Abbey Street, beside the Royal Oak (see item 25) at the narrow point in Long Street (Ordnance Survey map reference ST 666 012).

Abbey Street is to be taken slowly. You overdose in history as you pass between St Mary's Parish Church (see item 15) and the half-timbered Tudor houses that overhang the pavement (see item 27). You then pass the Stocks (see item 19) and the Congregational Chapel (see item 17), as you approach the Town Pond and the graceful mellow stone frontage of Abbey Farm, the Abbey's former South Gatehouse (see item 6) which looks down the street from the point where the Abbey precincts began.

Here, at the end of the street, just after the duck pond, you turn right through the front gate beneath the stone arch, and enter the churchyard. Follow the right-hand wall to the clump of trees. Below them, and always clear and flowing (though this is not to be taken as a recommendation to sample, given the proximity of burials) is Cerne's holy well, St Augustine's Well (see item 3). Toss in a coin for luck.

Then walk across the churchyard to the smaller arched gate, with a cross and shield carved into one of the jambs. "This Wall was Erected in 1838" a stone tells you. Through it passes Cerne Abbas footpath 3.

Walk into the field, the site of the mediaeval Cerne Abbey (see item 4), with the porch to the Abbot's Hall (see item 5) standing in the trees to the left. Walk diagonally across the field to the opposite corner. Beside the clump of trees you cross a stile, to join Cerne Abbas footpath 2.

This climbs the slope ahead of you, to the right of centre, and emerges from the trees to pass just below the feet of the Cerne Giant (see item 1). Follow the foot of the slope around the next corner of the hillside on to a more open expanse of sloping downland. Towards the far side there is a slight ledge cut into the hill and you walk up this to the summit, about half a mile north from the Giant. At the top are the banks and ditches of the Iron Age settlement where the builders of the Giant probably lived. Next comes an arable field.

Cross the stile and walk left of centre across this field to a barn immediately to the right of the small wood on the skyline. Walk between the trees and the barn, and then continue straight ahead, following the hedgerow and keeping it immediately on your left for a quarter of a mile.

Turn left through an iron hunting gate. This brings you on to Minterne Magna bridleway 8 which crosses the open hillside overlooking the upper Cerne valley. Follow it downhill, right of centre, through the gate and straight ahead on to a trackway that bends to the right and winds down the hill to a gate. You go through this into the field.

Walk straight across this field to join a farm track. This brings you to the hamlet about half a mile away, which is Minterne Parva. As you come to the garden of the first house you fork left, along an overgrown trackway, which is the continuation of Minterne Magna bridleway 9, and leads to barns and cottages at the end. You come out at a tarred unclassified public road, beside the stump of a mediaeval cross, and a circular granary.

Turn left along the road, and follow it to its junction with the main road (by the postbox). Here you turn left, for about a hundred yards, to the signpost at Port Knap.

Then turn right along the lane signposted "Up Cerne ½". After the thatched cottages you continue straight ahead across the village crossroads. Follow this road up the rise, passing the lawns of the Manor House, a fine building of 1601 which is equally impressive inside, with much oak panelling. Continue on the road down a slope between an avenue of trees. At the bottom the tarred road bends abruptly to the left.

Here you turn right along a stony track which is an unclassified and untarred public road. This climbs on to the downs. At the top, which is called Seldon Hill, a track bends to the left about 250 yards after the sycamore wood.

Turn left along it. This is Up Cerne bridleway 2, which you follow around its next corner as well, at the top of Wancombe Hill. Then, after the straight stretch, the bridleway leaves the tractor track and continues directly ahead across an arable field to the crest of the downs on Ball's Hill. Running from right to left across the top of the hill – with views over the Sydling valley – is a prehistoric ridgeway.

Turn left along the trackway, which is Sydling St Nicholas bridleway 5, and follow it southwards for three-quarters of a mile to the television relay mast.

Underneath the mast you turn left, into the field immediately before it, and follow the right-hand hedge for about 15 yards. This is Cerne Abbas footpath 27, which then continues straight ahead for 150 yards to the hazel coppice. This was Cerne's mediaeval deer park (see item 14). The park pale earthwork is visible beneath the hedge to your left and then strikes off across the field between Cerne Park woods and the television transmitter.

Turn right at this corner of the wood and walk 50 yards to the track into it. Then fork right and go downhill into the sheltered bowl of the valley, with the trees surrounding you, for a quarter of a mile. You come to a corner of a field and cross the stile into it, beside some fence rails. Head downhill, along the floor of the coombe, between Common Hill and Rowden Hill, towards Cerne. Cross the stiles beside the gates at the bottom of the hill and keep walking straight ahead, ignoring the more prominent track that leads towards a farmyard before the first gate.

Skirt the foot of the hillside. The path winds around the base of the slope and you keep a hedgerow immediately to your right. You go through a gate and along a track that is hemmed in on both sides by hedgerow and bushes. This path joins with a larger, dirt track and becomes Cerne Abbas bridleway 34 for its final 200 yards before coming out on to the main road beside Cerne's Victorian Workhouse (see item 21), the large three-storey slate-roofed building with an excellent view of the Giant. It is now a nursing home.

Turn right at the main road, and then left along the road signposted "Village Centre". About a hundred yards along this road, after the milestone but shortly before the "School" sign, there is a lane to your left.

Turn left along this short length of unclassified public road but only for about a hundred yards. Then turn right just before Kettle Bridge (see item 11) on to Millbank, which is a section of Cerne Abbas footpath 1 that runs beside the Cerne River.

As you reach the village houses, do not cross the footbridge but follow Cerne Abbas footpath 31, over a waterfall, into Mill Lane. At the end of the lane you turn left and come into Long Street, opposite the New Inn (see item 23).

Walk 2. Two-and-a-half-mile northern circuit, around Giant Hill.

Start from the Royal Oak (see item 25) and walk eastwards through the narrows of Long Street to the junction with Piddle Lane (the road to Piddletrenthide) but here you carry on along Alton Lane, which is signposted "Buckland Newton 4".

Proceed for a hundred yards, passing Simsay and The Lodge, to the metal gate with a kissing gate beside it.

Turn left here, into the field, and walk along Cerne Abbas footpath 4. It turns immediately right and follows the hedge to the corner. Turn left here and now keep the fence to your right. It brings you to a stile, to the right of a gate, and from here you walk up to the stile near the top right-hand corner of the next field. On the left are the earthwork remains of the wall that marked the precincts of the former Abbey Church (see item 4). This is Beaver Field (see item 12).

Cross the stile and turn left along Cerne Abbas bridleway 5 which bends to the right and climbs the hill diagonally in a half mile ascent from the 425 feet contour to 800 feet above sea level. The dry coombe beneath, to your right, is Yelcombe Bottom.

At the summit you follow a fence for 200 yards and then turn left at the two gates, on to Cerne Abbas bridleway 39. This heads towards the left-hand side of the wood, on the skyline in 200 yards, and you keep the fence to your right.

When you come to the track that branches off to the barn, beside the wood, you turn abruptly left and go in the opposite direction. Your course is where, at the time of writing, there is no visible path on the ground. You put your back to the trees and head directly across the middle of a large arabie field. Cerne Abbas footpath 2 goes in a straight line to a stile to the right of the main scrub-belt on the other side.

Cross the stile into the flora-rich expanse of open downland. Turn left and pass over the banks and ditches of an Iron Age through to Romano-British Celtic settlement that in all probability housed the creators of the Cerne Giant (see item 1). The path gradually descends the escarpment to pass beside the fence below the Giant's feet and then brings you into the trees.

On the other side of this clump you drop down to a wide droveway, but instead of crossing into this you continue straight ahead over the second, left-hand, stile, on to Cerne Abbas footpath 3. This parkland field is the site of the mediaeval Cerne Abbey (see item 4). You go down to the arched gate in the churchyard wall, in the right-hand corner. As you approach it, you pass the back of the Porch to the Abbot's Hall (see item 5) in the trees to your right. Next on your right is the monastic Guest-house (see item 7).

Having entered the churchyard, beneath the date-stone telling you "This Wall was Erected AD 1838", you walk straight ahead between the graves to the wall on the other side. Turn left here and walk down into the trees in the depression. At the foot is Cerne's holy well, St Augustine's Well (see item 3), which still has some hold on residual beliefs, to the extent of a few coins tossed in for luck.

Walk back up the path and follow it to the larger stone arch, with an iron gate, into Abbey Street. You emerge beside Abbey Farm which was formerly the monks' South Gate-house (see item 6). It is still the passageway to the Abbey Guest-house (see item 7) and the Porch (see item 5), but this path is not public and its availability depends upon whatever notices and charges apply. Bring some change for here, the well, and the parish church.

As for Abbey Street, after the Town Pond you pass the former Congregational Chapel (see item 17), which is set back on the right, the outstanding line of Tudor houses (see item 27), the Stocks (see item 19), and come to the door of St Mary's church (see item 15). The street ends with the Royal Oak (see item 25).

If your car is at the picnic area, you turn right along Long Street, and go right again at the corner, into Duck Street. Then go immediately right into Mill Lane which is Cerne Abbas footpath 31. This brings you to the River Cerne and Cerne Abbas footpath 1, known as Millbank, which follows the stream to Kettle Bridge.

Walk 3. Three mile southern circuit, around Black Hill.

Start from the eastern end of Long Street and turn south into Piddle Lane, which is signposted to Piddletrenthide (Ordnance Survey map reference ST 667 013). Walk along the lane for half a mile, up out of the village. After Stable Court there is a bend and the slope becomes steeper. Three hundred yards after the bend the beech trees on the right touch those of a second hillside wood, Piddle Wood, from the left side of the road.

Eighty yards before the point where the trees meet you turn right. Cross the carpet of dog's mercury in the hedgerow and climb a stile into the field.

Turn left along the slope of the downland escarpment and walk diagonally up it, along a sunken trackway which is Cerne Abbas footpath 12. Cross the stile beside a gate at the top corner of the hill pasture where the wire fence joins a hedgerow.

In thirty paces you turn left through a hunting gate and then turn right, now with the hedgerow to your right. Turn left at the end of the field, still keeping the hedge to your right. You come to a paddock fence.

Turn right across the stile in a hundred yards. Walk straight across the paddock and then keep the buildings of Black Hill Farm to your right.

Immediately after the garden of the bungalow you turn right and follow the farm track downhill. Keep the factory farm to your right.

You are walking Cerne Abbas footpath 11 which brings you to the head of a deep-cut dry valley. Turn left into it, just below the slurry tank. Shortly after the gate the track that enters the valley swings sharply right and then forks left. Tree clearing, in about 1980, was sympathetic rather than total and has created an impression of parkland.

The path runs down the valley floor of Bramble Bottom, which becomes arable, for half a mile. Cross the second fence-line at a stile left of centre towards the foot of the left-hand downland escarpment. Walk in the strip of old woodland between the hedges, with the hill to your left and a field to the right. In 300 yards, at the corner, you go to the right of the hedge-belt and walk in the arable field. Now keep the hedge to your left.

In another 300 yards or so you leave the next field and turn right on to a tractor road that approaches the silos of Pound Farm, in a further 300 yards.

On entering the farmyard you turn right on to Cerne Abbas footpath

14. Walk up past the house and bungalow, which are to your left. You are heading up the valley, with water-meadows to the left, and go through a gate. This long field is dominated by the slope of Green Hill which rises sharply to the right.

Leave by the gate in the middle of the hedge at the far end of the field, about a hundred yards above the site of old watercress beds. Walk right of centre across this next field, going diagonally to the top right-hand corner. Here the path goes through the fence into the scrubby downland at the foot of Black Hill escarpment.

Turn left. The public path runs above or beside the left-hand hedgerow for a third of a mile before you pass under electricity cables, cross two stiles, and enter a field above Cerne's allotments. The hedgerow is now to your right for a hundred yards.

Instead of crossing the next stile you turn left and walk down beside the allotments, which you keep to your left, and go straight ahead along the tarred road, which is Chescombe.

Turn right at the road junction, along Back Street. Proceed for a hundred yards.

Then turn left into Cerne Abbas footpath 29, sandwiched between Eleanor and house No.13, on the left side of the street thirty yards before Abbots Walk. This alleyway cuts through to the eastern end of Long Street.

4. Four mile south-western circuit, around Dickley Hill.

Start from The Folly, which is the street that extends westwards from Long Street, and bridges the River Cerne (Ordnance Survey map reference ST 664 011) between a couple of low stone walls on a wide, flat piece of road. Turn left fifty yards west of the bridge, opposite Barton Lodge, on to Cerne Abbas footpath 17 which goes through a wooden hunting gate next to the main gate to the central drive.

The path skirts the left-hand side of the grounds, close to the stream, and does not go up the drive to Barton Farm, which is to the right. This magnificent building on the other side of the lawn, to your right, is the 130 feet surviving length of the Abbey's Tithe Barn – the end towards The Folly used to extend a further seventy feet (see item 8).

At the end of the garden the path crosses a stile and you walk right of centre over the low earthworks in the water-meadows, which are probably the remains of monastic fish-ponds, to a gate near the far right-hand corner of the field. Turn left on the other side and cross the stile to continue straight ahead across the arable field and go through a pair of gates that are right of centre in the double fences on the other side.

Proceed across the next field to the roadside stile near the far right-hand corner.

Turn left along the main road, for 700 yards. On the other side of the rise you pass a track that leads to the sewage works. You continue along the road to the next pair of gates, on the right-hand side.

Turn right here and walk along Cerne Abbas footpath 21 which rises gently up the arable Higher Hill Bottom for half a mile before going through a gate on to the downland escarpment. Go to the left of the barn at Oakham Close and then straight ahead up the steep slope in front of you. Aim for the left-hand side of the beech clump at the top.

Here there is a stile, to the left of the ruins of Large Bar Barn.

Cross a short strip of arable field, walking straight across to the hedgerow. On the other side of the hedge, by crossing a stile, you come to the prehistoric Ridgeway path, which in these parts is now Sydling St Nicholas bridleway 5.

Turn right along it for 500 yards, heading towards the bungalow and barn in the near distance, and the television relay mast beyond.

Give a backward glance to the hilltop immediately above the valley path up which you have just walked. You are standing at the 700 feet contour and can glimpse the waves and troughs of some earthworks half a mile away on the downland spur that juts out towards the main Cerne valley. This spot is as near as the public path network comes to a view of those banks and ditches on Smacam Down which comprise a major Romano-British settlement surrounded by native field systems. In their midst is the five foot high bank of a wedge-shaped Neolithic long barrow, a communal burial mound which pre-dates the settlement remains by more than three millennia, dating from about 3,500 BC.

Put your back to the earthworks and head for a more recent landmark, the television relay mast. In 500 yards you come to a tarred road and cross to the hillside track that continues on the other side.

In a third of a mile it bends to the right and then to the left. A hundred yards after this second bend, about 300 yards before the television mast, you turn right through the hedge and enter the field. You are at the head of a splendid wooded valley, which is known as Cerne Park, enclosed by and preserving the name of the monks' mediaeval deer park (see item 14). Cerne Abbas footpath 23 goes straight ahead into the field for a hundred yards and then turns right to cross the rounded southern edge of the park. Make sure that you keep above the woodland.

The dense hedgerow to your right is the Park Pale and you re-cross it at the second gap. This is 300 yards from the oil tank where it joins the Ridgeway hedgerow.

The path now becomes a farm track. Walk over the rise, following the line of power cables.

Turn left at the buildings and walk across the arable slope, down to a gate. You enter a chalky grassland coombe, which is Park Mead Bottom.

Turn right, to follow the right-hand hedgerow, and cross the fence. Continue around the top of the valley to the road on the side of Dickley Hill.

Turn left and walk down Sydling Road into Cerne. You pass Cerne Park Farm, Park Lodge, Mount Pleasant Farm, Barton House Farm, and the attractive flint and brick 1987-built town houses of Acreman Close.

Go straight over at the crossroads into The Folly. If, however, your car is in Duck Street or at the picnic area you turn left along Acreman Street and then right into Wills Lane which comes out midway along Duck Street, beside the school. Turn left for the picnic site, and then right after the road narrows.

TRADESMENS TOKEN

Arms on the Gate-house at Cerne Abbas.

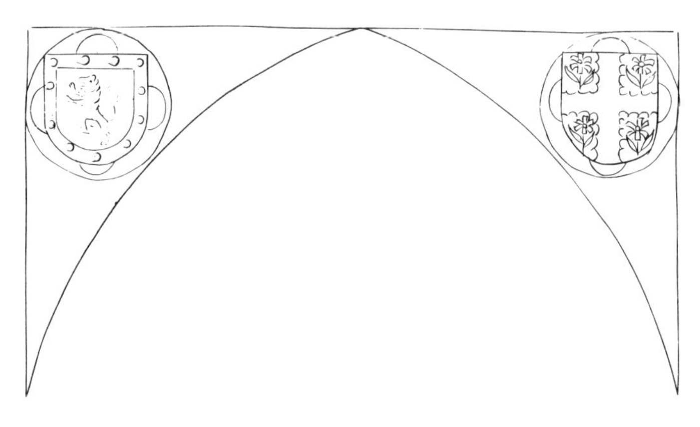

ROUTE MAP
for the four CERNE WALKS

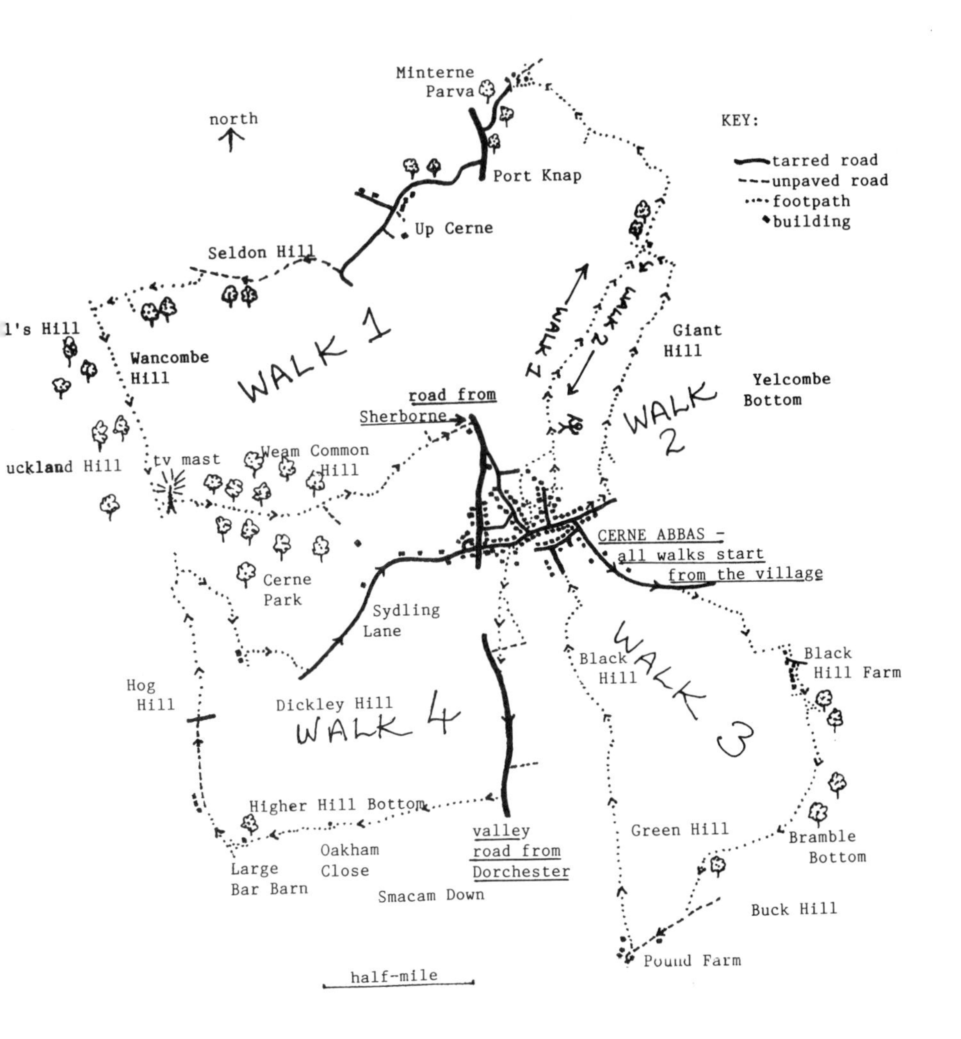

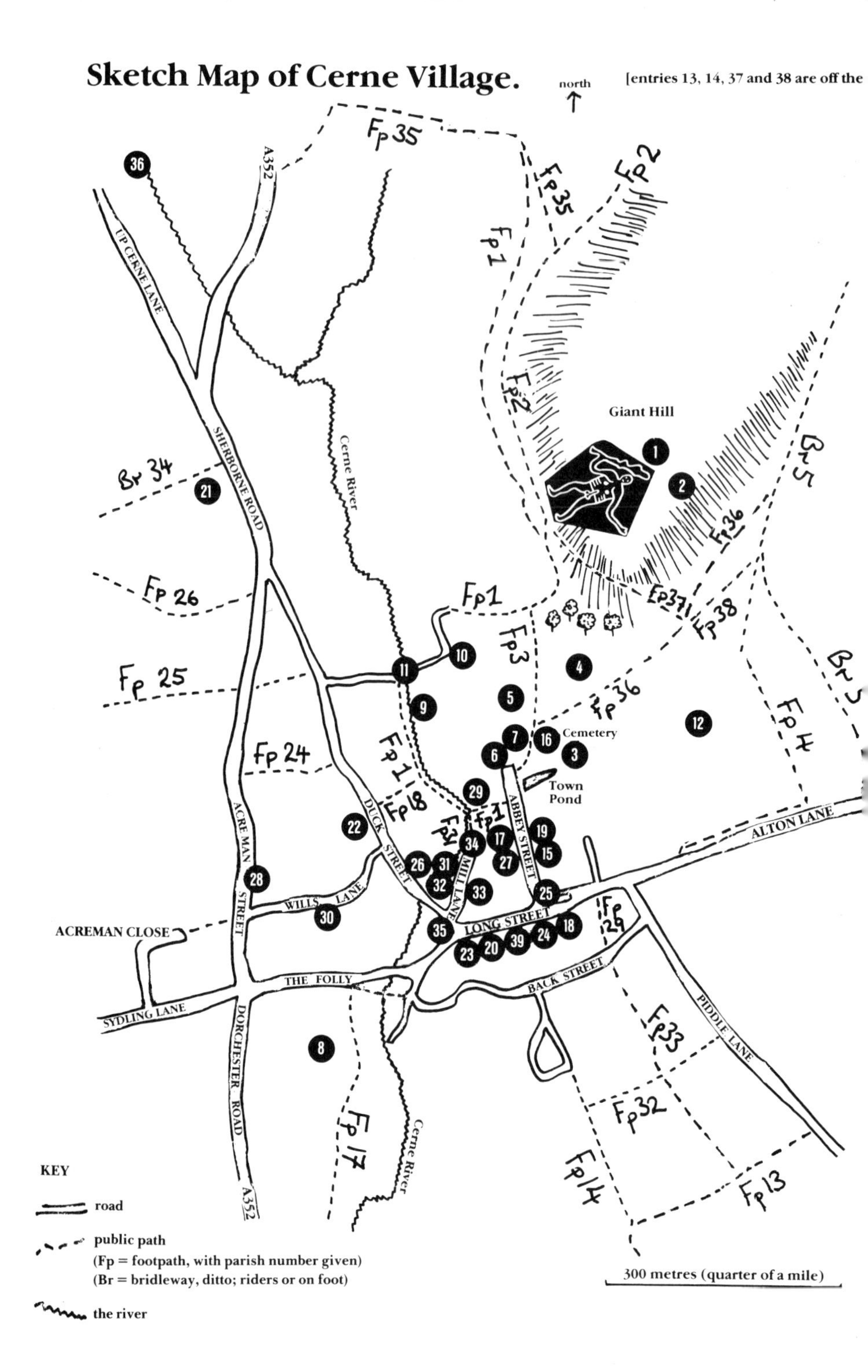

Sketch Map of Cerne Village.
north
[entries 13, 14, 37 and 38 are off the
Fp 35
A352
Fp 2
Fp 1
UP CERNE LANE
Fp 2
Giant Hill
SHERBORNE ROAD
Cerne River
Br 34
Br 5
Fp 36
Fp 26
Fp 1
Fp 37
Fp 38
Fp 3
Fp 25
Fp 36
Br 5
Cemetery
Fp 4
Fp 24
Fp 1
Town
Pond
Fp 18
Fp 1
ABBEY STREET
DUCK STREET
ALTON LANE
ACRE MAN
STREET
MILL LANE
WILLS LANE
Fp 29
ACREMAN CLOSE
LONG STREET
THE FOLLY
BACK STREET
SYDLING LANE
DORCHESTER ROAD
PIDDLE LANE
Fp 33
Fp 32
Fp 17
Cerne River
Fp 14
Fp 13
A352
KEY
road
public path
(Fp = footpath, with parish number given)
(Br = bridleway, ditto; riders or on foot)
the river
300 metres (quarter of a mile)